TEXAS ALLIGATORS

A Wildlife Profile

TEXAS ALLIGATORS
A Wildlife Profile

Darlene Prescott

*This book is dedicated to
my teenage grandniece,
Mia Louise Arcangeli,
who deserves to continue living in
a world of rich and diverse wildlife.*

High Island•Photo credit: William H. Powell

TABLE OF CONTENTS

Acknowledgments

I am grateful to the people at the Texas Parks and Wildlife Department (TPWD) for their assistance and permission to use their extensive digital and print resources.

Mr. Amos Cooper, TPWD's alligator program leader, assisted me as I researched and wrote this book. I am indebted to him for his expertise and time, and especially for reviewing the manuscript.

I am appreciative of Ms. Monique Slaughter, former biologist for the TPWD's alligator program, and of Dr. Valentine Lance, member of the Crocodile Specialist Group of the International Union for Conservation of Nature and Adjunct Professor of Biology at San Diego State University. They took the time to read the manuscript and offered expert advice on an early draft.

I must also thank Dr. Mark E. Merchant, Professor of Biochemistry at McNeese State University in Lake Charles, Louisiana, for providing me with information on alligator research and helping me understand it. Dr. Merchant also reviewed the manuscript and offered valuable advice.

Dr. Edward L. Braun, Associate Professor of Biology at the University of Florida and member of the International Crocodilian Genomes Working Group, was helpful in providing me with information on the genome-sequencing process of the American alligator.

There are others who helped me along the way, including Dr. Llewellyn D. Densmore at Texas Tech University; Dr. Ruth M. Elsey at the Rockefeller Wildlife Refuge in Grand Chenier, Louisiana; Mr. Brian Hill at the Houston Zoo; Mr. Mark Kramer at the Armand Bayou Nature Center in Pasadena, Texas; Dr. Wade Alan Ryberg at Texas A&M University; and Mr. Jim Stinebaugh, Special Agent, Law Enforcement, at the U.S. Fish and Wildlife Service in Houston, Texas.

FOREWORD

At a 2013 meeting of the United Nations Commission on Crime Prevention and Criminal Justice, the United States and Peru put forward a resolution urging countries to impose stricter penalties for wildlife trafficking.

The resolution, which was passed by the commission members, recognizes the illicit trafficking of wildlife fauna and flora as a "serious crime," and recommends that it be treated as such by all nations.

Protection of wildlife—which includes protection of wildlife habitats—was acknowledged not only as necessary to the survival of endangered species, but also as important to the economic sustainability of many countries around the world.

World leaders seem to agree that without wild creatures like tigers, rhinoceroses, and alligators, life on Planet Earth would be far less interesting.

I. Distribution

If you are in or next to a body of water in the eastern parts of Texas, you may very well find yourself near a wild American alligator, or *Alligator mississippiensis*—the only crocodilian native to Texas. Although Texas has lost most of its wilderness, its alligator population is rising.

The highest concentration of American alligators in Texas is found in the far southeastern corner of the state, but alligators can be found in approximately 125 of the state's 254 counties. Its habitat extends from the Sabine River to the Gulf of Mexico, across the coastal marshes to the Rio Grande, and west to around Interstate Highway 35.

Alligators in four East Texas counties number around 250,000, and Chambers County has 100,000 of them.

While the alligator is more prevalent in the southeastern part of Texas, you will find a small population in the Rio Grande Valley—including in the Rio Grande River. Generally, the state's coastal gator population ends around Corpus Christi, so this somewhat isolated population is curious. However, the Rio Grande Valley is not really a valley, but rather a floodplain made up of oxbow lakes and resacas, formed from cut-off channels from earlier courses of the Rio Grande River. In other words, the area has enough water habitats in which to support a gator population, but the question remains on how the reptile moved into the area. There are stories of people in the past releasing pet alligators into the local bodies of water—and one story of a zoo donating some to a state park. The alligator also could have traveled down to the Valley using the Gulf Intracoastal Waterway—which flows from the East Coast, through the southern coastal states, into Texas. The Waterway ends at the Port of Brownsville, which is located near the river mouth of the Rio Grande.

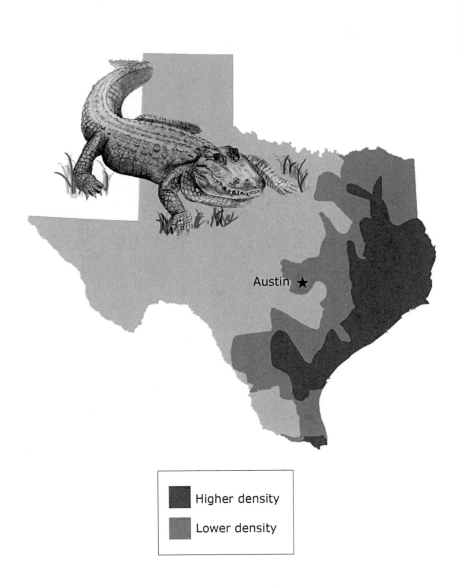

Austin ★

Higher density
Lower density

Distribution of alligators in Texas•Illustration credit: Sandra Lorenzo

The range of *Alligator mississippiensis* in the United States is bound by Texas in the west, and up to North Carolina on the eastern coast. The states in between include Alabama, Arkansas, Florida, Georgia, Louisiana, Mississippi, Oklahoma, and South Carolina. Of the ten states that have wild alligator populations, Louisiana has the largest and Oklahoma the smallest.

Cold temperatures generally keep alligators south of the thirtieth parallel north. These reptiles can, and do, live outside of tropical climates, but they cannot tolerate severe or prolonged periods of cold weather.

Alligators, crocodiles, caimans, and gharials are all included in the crocodilian group. There are 23 crocodilian species in existence today: two alligators, 14 crocodiles, five caimans, and two gharials.

The Chinese alligator (*Alligator sinensis*) is found in freshwater marshes along the Yangtze River in eastern China, which is on the thirtieth parallel north, giving it the same northern range as the American alligator. Chinese alligators are smaller than their American counterparts, usually not more than five feet long, and they have a shorter snout. They are very rare, but captive breeding programs in zoos and research facilities around the world are helping keep the species alive.

The American crocodile, or *Crocodylus acutus*, is the only crocodile in North America. It is found in the Florida Everglades and the Florida Keys, as well as in parts of the Caribbean, Mexico, Central America, and northern South America. It has been classified as threatened in Florida, but the population is growing. There are over a dozen other species of crocodiles living in the more tropical areas of the world.

The caiman is relatively small, usually less than eight feet long, and is found in southern Mexico, Central America, and South America. The gharial, which has a long, slender snout, is native to the Indian subcontinent, and is one of the most endangered animals in the world.

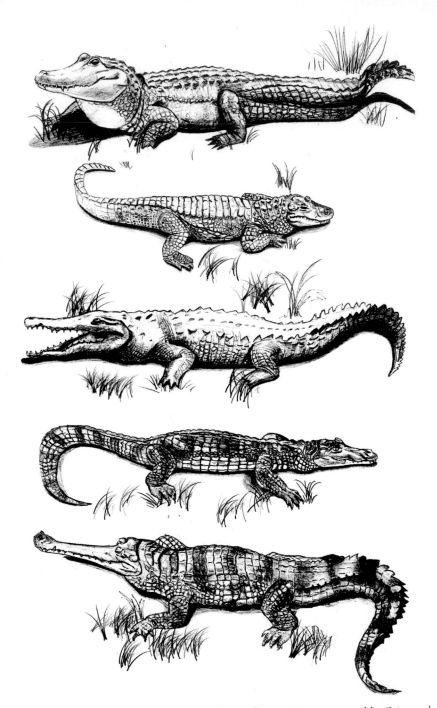

From top to bottom: American alligator, Chinese alligator, American crocodile, Caiman & Gharial•Illustration credit: Sandra Lorenzo

The alligator population of any given area will fluctuate, depending on hurricanes and droughts. Hurricane Ike in 2008, as well as drought conditions during the summer of 2011, forced alligators in Texas to move farther north. Warming trends may continue to expand the northern range of alligators, as long as suitable wetlands are available.

Several methods are presently used to estimate alligator populations. Aerial surveys of nests and night eye-shine counts of alligators in bodies of water are the most popular techniques, and are used every year to survey the Texas population. Another method is to count basking alligators. Aerial nest surveys are considered the most accurate.

II. Habitat

Alligators, like all crocodilians, live mostly in water, so the preservation of enough wetlands to allow the animals to roam and reproduce undisturbed is crucial. Texas wetlands are a valuable resource, not only for alligators and other wildlife, but also for flood protection, water quality, and the overall economy of the state. Over the past two hundred years, Texas wetlands have been drained, filled, and used as dumps. Since the 1970s, however, the Texas Parks and Wildlife Department, U.S. Fish and Wildlife Service, U.S. Environmental Protection Agency, and the Texas General Land Office have supported wetlands protection and restoration. The U.S. Army Corps of Engineers also has programs.

Anahuac National Wildlife Refuge•Photo credit: A. Brinly

Alligators in Texas can be found in its rivers, lakes, ponds, canals, bayous, swamps, and coastal marshes. You will also find them in the gator holes and dens they dig.

Most Texas alligators live in freshwater, intermediate, and brackish marshes along the Gulf Coast, and in bayous, swamps, and wetlands in East Texas. Marshes that have been diked for mosquito control, oil exploration, or water management are still suitable for alligators. Alligators in Texas are flourishing in the maze-like coastal refuges of such dikes or levees. Typically, one finds males in deeper water and females in shallower freshwater marshes.

Brazos Bend State Park•Photo credit: A. Brinly

Occasionally, larger alligators will enter saltwater habitats, but smaller gators cannot tolerate this very well. Prolonged exposure to saltwater dehydrates these reptiles, and there is some evidence that alligators that ingest a steady intake of saltwater undergo physiological changes that make them unable to eat. The flooding of coastal waters with saltwater due to hurricanes, therefore, puts alligator populations at risk and forces them farther inland for fresher water.

Estero Llano Grande State Park•Photo credit: William H. Powell

Horsepen Bayou•Photo credit: A. Brinly

Such saltwater surges also kill marsh vegetation and many of the animals that alligators feed on. After the storm surge from Hurricane Ike in 2008 damaged alligator habitats in coastal marshes along the upper Texas coast, many alligators died, and the following spring was one of the worst nesting seasons on record.

Drought also affects alligator populations. The lack of flushing rainfall during the summer of 2011 kept salinity levels high, and the Texas Parks and Wildlife Department reported significant losses.

Alligators, however, are highly resilient and can recover over time. After Hurricane Katrina in 2005, for example, the Louisiana alligator population had reached near normal levels within a few years.

When there are no large bodies of water in an area, an alligator may dig a hole near a swamp or a riverbank that allows water to seep in. These gator holes vary greatly in width and depth and can take years to dig. Gator holes become homes to fish and turtles, and in periods of drought may hold the only water in the area.

During dry spells and cold weather, alligators build dens in riverbanks or near their gator holes. The dens are big enough that the gator can turn around and face the entrance. Alligators also build dens, or caves, that are reached by underwater entrances. The animal digs a tunnel underwater and fashions the den at the end of the tunnel above water level.

It is important to keep in mind that a body of water may not contain an alligator one day, but could have one the next day. Alligators move around not only to escape salty water and drought conditions, but also to locate food and mates. Young, growing alligators move away from adult alligators in order to avoid attack. One of the author's cousins was surprised one day when he visited his farm pond in Crosby, Texas, and discovered that a medium-sized gator had moved in.

In whatever habitat you find alligators, you will also find the benefits they afford. In addition to providing homes for other water-loving animals, alligators play a key role in managing the ecology of a wetlands area. Gators keep the small mammal population under control and offer protection to heron and egret rookeries. The birds build nests above alligator habitats to avoid raids by opossums and raccoons. Turtles may also lay their eggs in alligator nests, where mulch piles and other nesting materials keep the eggs warm. When the young turtles hatch, they crawl toward the water, just as the gator hatchlings do. Of course, the mother alligator will eat any bird or turtle it catches.

III. Anatomy & Function

The American alligator—and the American crocodile—are the largest reptiles in North America. The alligator shares many characteristics with other reptiles, but has some anatomical features that non-crocodilian reptiles do not have.

Armand Bayou•Photo credit: A. Brinly

All crocodilians are carnivorous and look like armed lizards. They depend on strong muscles to catch prey and tough hides for defense. Indeed, their muscles and hides account for most of their body weight.

ALLIGATOR SKIN

The hide of the alligator is very tough and is formed of rectangular scales. The horny scales are called scutes, and those containing bone are known as osteoderms. The creamy white, unarmored scales under the throat, on the belly, and under the tail have no scutes, and are typically the parts of the hide that are turned into wallets and handbags.

Armand Bayou•Photo credit: A. Brinly

The alligator is the darkest of all crocodilians. Their grayish-black skin helps them blend into their surroundings, and their prey often does not see them until it is too late. Alligators that live in the northeastern part of Texas tend to have more coloring than coastal alligators, due to differences in their diets.

White alligators exist, but are very rare, and can only survive in captivity because of their sensitivity to sunlight and their visibility to predators. There are two types of white alligators: albino and leucistic. Albino alligators have a nonfunctional gene for melanin. In leucistic alligators, which are white with blue eyes, all pigment genes are defective, not just the melanin gene. You can see one of these alligators at the Houston Zoo; Blanco is one of about a dozen leucistic alligators on exhibit around the world.

The Magnificent Head

The easiest way to distinguish an alligator from a crocodile is to compare the alligator's more rounded snout to the crocodile's more pointed snout.

Anahuac National Wildlife Refuge•Photo credit: William H. Powell

Alligators have powerful jaws—powerful enough to hold onto large, struggling prey. However, while they have tremendous strength for closing their jaws, the muscles to reopen them are much weaker. This means that a person can hold an alligator's jaws shut, rendering them almost impossible to open.

The hollow, conical teeth of the alligator are designed solely for holding prey; it has no molars for crushing or grinding. When the reptile twists its entire body, it is able to tear off parts of its prey for consumption. The teeth are replaced as they break off unless the animal is very old. When an alligator closes its jaws, only some of the upper teeth are typically visible, because the lower teeth fit into sockets in its upper jaw. This contrasts with the crocodile's lower teeth, some of which are visible when its jaws are closed. The alligator has 80 teeth: 40 on top and 40 on the bottom.

The inner lining of the alligator's mouth is soft tissue, and varies in color from pinkish to yellowish. The tongue is attached to the floor of the mouth and does not protrude. The alligator has a flap at the back of its mouth that covers the throat opening, preventing water from entering the lungs when the animal opens its mouth underwater.

Brazos Bend State Park•Photo credit: A. Brinly

Alligators have two musk glands under the lower jaw and two in the cloaca, the outer opening of the intestinal, urinary, and genital tracts. The function of these glands is not completely understood.

Crocodilians have larger brains than most reptiles, but in general they are not as large as those of birds or mammals. The brain does possess a small cerebral cortex that controls conscious thought, which is evidence that these animals can learn. For example, in areas where they are frequently hunted, alligators learn to hide at the sight of a searchlight or the sound of a boat.

THE ALLIGATOR HAS EXCELLENT SIGHT, HEARING, AND SMELL.

The eyes of the alligator have a wide field of vision. The irises of young alligators are green and turn brown as they age. Alligators have two sets of eyelids. The inner lids are transparent and close from back to front, which protect the eyes underwater, and the outer set is made of skin and closes top to bottom like those of humans.

Horsepen Bayou•Photo credit: A. Brinly

Alligators can see very well at night, which is when they do much of their hunting. Their vertical, catlike pupils open wide to allow light to enter in low-light situations. At the back of the retina,

Horsepen Bayou•Photo credit: A. Brinly

a reflective layer called the tapetum reflects light back through the pupil, increasing the reptile's ability to see in the dark. The tapetum causes the eyes to reflect red when bright light is directed at the gator.

The ears of an alligator are not prominent. They are located behind the eyes and are covered with a skin flap that keeps out water. Alligators have well-developed middle-ear bones, unlike other reptiles.

The alligator's two nasal openings are located at the tip of its snout, and have crescent-shaped flaps of skin that close over the openings underwater.

ALLIGATOR COMMUNICATION

The alligator is quite vocal compared to the crocodile. With its jaws shut, the gator blows out its breath in a series of long, rumbling roars that can be heard for half a mile or more. If the bellowing takes place in the water, the vibrations can set the water around the animal in motion. Both the adult male and the female bellow, but the male's bellows are slower than the female's. Naturalists are not sure why alligators do this, but they speculate that it may simply be to announce their presence and to warn off juvenile males. Bellowing occurs most frequently in April and May, during breeding season.

Alligators make popping noises by slapping the surface of the water with their heads, more frequently as mating season approaches. Gators will make hissing sounds, which are thought to be a warning to stay away.

Alligators also communicate by merely watching each other. Large, powerful alligators force smaller ones to give up sunning spots on the bank or resting places in shallow water. Often there is no physical contact between individual animals; just the presence of a large alligator is enough to send the message to the smaller animal that it must give way—or suffer the consequences.

ALLIGATORS HAVE A HEART!

While amphibians and most other reptiles have two-chambered hearts, crocodilians have four-chambered hearts like humans. The four-chambered heart provides for more efficient blood circulation, and allows the alligator to hold its breath and swim for extended periods. When the animal is submerged, blood is routed through the heart to bypass the lungs. Bypassing the lungs conserves oxygen for the rest of the organs.

The alligator spends a lot of time floating on the surface of the water. By regulating the amount of air in its lungs, the animal can float or sink just below the surface, with only its eyes and nose above the water.

Brazos Bend State Park•Photo credit: A. Brinly

REGULATION OF BODY TEMPERATURE

Like other reptiles, alligators are cold-blooded, or ectothermic, meaning that the air or water temperature around them determines their body temperature. If an alligator becomes cool, it must lie in the sun to raise its temperature to a level that permits it to move around. If it becomes too hot, it will lie on the bank with its mouth open. Moisture evaporating in the reptile's large mouth cools the blood moving through the mouth tissue. The alligator will also slide into the water to cool off.

Armand Bayou•Photo credit: A. Brinly

Alligators are able to stand colder temperatures for longer periods of time than any other crocodilian, but do become less active when temperatures reach 60°F or colder. However, most alligators, like other crocodilians, live in relatively warm regions, and this means that the alligator expends little energy maintaining a high body temperature. Most of the animal's food, therefore, becomes energy for growth and movement.

Temperature is also correlated with how long an alligator can remain underwater. On warm days, alligators can stay underwater at least 45 minutes. In cooler weather, when their metabolic rates are slower, they can remain submerged much longer. An alligator's activity level also affects the amount of time it can remain submerged; if the alligator is moving around, it must surface more often for air. And a larger alligator can stay underwater longer than a smaller one.

MOBILITY

The alligator has a powerful tail, which it uses in a side-to-side motion to swim and to catapult itself out of the water.

Not only is the alligator an excellent swimmer, moving as fast as six miles per hour in the water, but it can also move quickly on land for short distances. In fact, alligators can run as fast as an adult human. It moves by sliding or walking, and sometimes

Brazos Bend State Park•Photo credit: A. Brinly

raises itself high off the ground for short bursts of movement. It also has a galloping gait. The animal's energy can be explosive, but it cannot sustain bursts for long periods.

A little-known fact is that gators' front feet have five toes, while the webbed back feet have four each. Sharp claws are found on most of the toes, except for the fourth and fifth outer toes on the front feet and the fourth outer toe on the back feet.

Male and female alligators usually have separate, individual territories. The female tends to remain close to her nesting area, but the male wanders more, especially during breeding season.

FINDING FOOD

Alligators are highly predatory, opportunistic hunters that will eat almost anything. They are also cannibalistic—large alligators will eat smaller ones.

Alligators eat, grow, and burn calories when the weather is warm and food is plentiful, but reduce activity to a minimum for months at a time if temperatures turn cold and the food supply diminishes. The alligator is also able to store fat in its tail for periods of famine.

The alligator's cold-blooded, slower metabolism has aided in its long-term survival. Smaller alligators have higher metabolic rates, so they eat more often, but consume less volume at a time. By contrast, humans and other mammals require a fixed rate of energy to survive, so we must eat a certain amount every day to remain healthy.

Alligators usually hunt in the water, mostly between dusk and dawn, where they single out a victim and stalk it. Sensors on the sides of their snouts pick up scents and detect pressure changes to help them locate prey in the water. Once the alligator is close enough, it suddenly raises its head out of the water to attack. Other tactics are to remain in place and wait for prey to come to it, or to swim up from underneath the prey animal and try and swallow it whole.

Illustration credit: Sandra Lorenzo

Alligators also go after prey on land. Large alligators have been known to lie just below the water, waiting for a deer or cow to come to drink. Then with incredible speed, the gator grabs the prey by its nose or leg and drags it into deeper water until it drowns. Large animals may be dragged around or guarded for several days until the meat rots enough to be ripped apart.

The alligator tries to catch its prey with the side of its jaws, rather than head on, for a better grip. Then the reptile rips off parts of the prey animal in order to swallow it. The alligator cannot chew its food as the upper jaw is not flexible.

The alligator's digestive system is fairly simple, and consists of a two-part stomach and an intestine that ends in the cloaca. The gizzard-like first section of the stomach crushes larger pieces, and the second lobe secretes strong digestive juices to digest the food. In fact, crocodilians have some of the strongest stomach acid known to vertebrates. The reptiles are able to digest bone. It takes about two days for food to leave both lobes of the stomach. Digestion time depends on what has been eaten, but in a warm, captive environment, an alligator can process a normal-sized meal, from eating to excretion, in three to five days.

Crocodilians swallow hard objects, such as pebbles and pieces of wood. Naturalists disagree on the reason for this behavior, but most believe that these gastroliths help grind the food in their stomachs.

ALLIGATOR RESEARCH

It has been observed that, although wild alligators often engage in violent territorial behavior and injurious encounters with other animals in bacteria-infested waters, they seldom develop fatal infections. Some herpetologists believe their strong immune systems may contribute to their long-term success.

Preliminary research has revealed that alligator blood contains powerful antibiotic properties that can kill a vast range of bacteria and fungi. Dr. Mark Merchant, a biochemistry professor at McNeese State University in Lake Charles, Louisiana, has isolated a specific protein in the alligator's white blood cells that contains antimicrobial properties—that could provide medical benefits for humans and other animals. Much of his research on alligators is taking place at the J. D. Murphree Wildlife Management Area in Port Arthur, Texas. Dr. Merchant has also obtained a patent to use gator blood as a food supplement for piglets that allows them to be weaned faster and more successfully than with a traditional diet.

Alligator skin is considered a good source of collagen, as it is composed mostly of that substance, and gator fat is being researched as a source of biodiesel fuel. With the knowledge that using soybeans and other food crops to produce biodiesel fuel raises the price of food, scientists have shown in laboratory experiments

Dr. Merchant extracting a blood sample from an alligator at the J.D. Murphree Wildlife Management Area•Photo credit: Troy Merchant

that oil extracted from alligator fat (which is typically discarded) can easily be converted into biodiesel fuel, and that such fuel is similar in composition to soybean biodiesel.

Scientists have recently completed the sequencing of the alligator's genome, which will tell us more about the animal's evolution and biochemistry, as well as result in further useful biological and biomedical research. As Dr. Edward Braun of the International Crocodilian Genomes Working Group explains, there are two steps in uncovering a genome: sequencing, then putting the sequences together. Work on the latter step is proceeding.

More research is needed to fully understand this ancient reptile and the benefits it could provide to humans, animals, and the environment. The American alligator has been used as a model for examining the environmental impact of contaminants in wild habitats. Further research may also rationalize the inconsistencies in the literature on the alligator.

IV. Life Cycle

MATING

Alligators in Texas are mostly inactive from mid-October until temperatures begin to rise in early March. They become more active in early March, and their mating behaviors coincide with warmer weather in April and May. By the end of May, breeding and nesting peak. Alligators begin mating when they grow to at least six feet.

Other environmental conditions factor into breeding behavior. Drought conditions, for example, stress alligators, and prevent many females from developing the hormones necessary to ovulate and breed.

Although male and female alligators have well-established pecking orders, they tolerate each other more easily during courting season. Usually, the female will swim to the male. As courtship progresses, the pair will begin to swim next to each other, sometimes touching noses or necks. They will sun together. The female may permit the male to stroke her back with his forelimb. The male may submerge underwater and blow a stream of bubbles past the female's head. Eventually, the female, while swimming beside the male, bends her tail upward and both submerge. Copulation takes place underwater—the act lasting approximately 30 seconds.

Large males may mate with several females during the season, and there is evidence that females also mate with multiple partners. DNA studies offer proof that multiple males often fertilize one female.

NESTING

Approximately two months after mating, depending on the temperature, female alligators build their nests. Young females generally nest every other year and lay fewer eggs than mature ones, and very old alligators do not nest at all. Females generally nest in the same vicinity from year to year, but the actual nest site is seldom reused.

South Padre Island Birding and Nature Center gator nest•Photo credit: Darlene Prescott

The female usually builds her nest 10 to 15 feet away from the water. The nest is cone-shaped, and most are three feet high and four to six feet wide at the bottom. The alligator builds the nest using vegetation in the area, and makes it high enough to keep the eggs from being flooded by fluctuations in the water level. Nest-building usually takes two to three days, with much of the work done at night. A path may be visible from the nest to the water, made by the female alligator coming and going.

At the top of the nest mound, she digs out a cavity with her hind feet and lays an egg every 30 to 45 seconds. The female lays between 15 and 60 eggs, depending on her size, age, and condition. Afterwards, she pushes more vegetation over the eggs, which are called a clutch.

Alligator eggs are bright white and oval in shape. They are the same size at both ends, and measure about three inches long and one and three-fourths inches wide. The hard outer shell is thicker than a chicken's egg, and the inner shell is a thick membrane.

Unlike birds, alligators do not have to sit on their nests to incubate their eggs, because the damp, decaying vegetation insulates the eggs from changes in temperature and humidity. Generally, temperatures inside the nest are slightly cooler than outside during the day, and slightly warmer at night.

Gender is determined by the temperature inside the nest during a ten-day period in the middle third of the incubation period; alligators do not possess sex chromosomes. Internal nest temperatures above 89°F usually produce all males, and cooler temperatures produce either both genders or all females. In the wild, nests are frequently warmer at the top than on the sides and bottom, so males develop in the upper layers and females from lower positions.

The instinct for females to guard their nests may be stronger at the beginning of the incubation period than at the end. Some stray during midsummer and return around the time the eggs hatch. Others remain near the nest site for the duration. If the nest is left unguarded, it may be raided by hogs, raccoons, rats, or other animals.

Hatchlings

The eggs hatch in late August and early September, about 65 days after being laid. The eggshell degrades as calcium is absorbed from the shell by the embryo. Just before hatching, a tiny egg tooth, or caruncle, develops at the end of the hatchling's snout. The egg tooth is a tough piece of epidermis that helps the hatchling tear through the inner shell after the outer shell begins to crack. It falls off shortly after hatching.

If she is still around, the mother hears her hatchlings' high-pitched grunts from up to 20 or 30 feet away, and she may come to help dig them out of the nest. However, most hatchlings are able to find

Anahuac National Wildlife Refuge•Photo credit: William H. Powell

their way out, and they instinctively head for the water. Hatchlings deep in the nest may not be able to free themselves and will perish. When a baby alligator reaches the water, it stays with its group, which is then called a pod.

Horsepen Bayou•Photo credit: A. Brinly

Anahuac National Wildlife Refuge•Photo credit: William H. Powell

Horsepen Bayou•Photo credit: A. Brinly

•*Illustration credit: Sandra Lorenzo*

Hatchlings are about eight to ten inches long when they hatch. They are born black with yellow cross bands on their backs, but they lose these bands and become more uniform in color as they grow, completely losing the bands at three to four years.

Hatchlings instinctively know how to swim, and immediately start looking for food, such as tadpoles, bugs, and spiders. The baby alligators' teeth are needle-sharp at this stage.

The baby alligators may remain in their mother's territory for one to three years before they go looking for their own. The mother tolerates them, and, if a hatchling gives a distress call (which sounds like the barking of a small puppy), she may answer it—and so might every other mature alligator in the area. Naturalists are not sure whether the alligators rush to help the young gator or to eat it, or perhaps even to eat the baby's predator.

Many hatchlings do not survive their first weeks because wading birds and raccoons eat them. Young alligators lead risky lives—much of their feeding is done in shallow water where larger animals can easily catch them.

GROWTH

If a young alligator manages to survive to the age of four or until it is four feet long, it is safe from predators. At around this time, its voice changes and both males and females will begin to bellow instead of grunt.

Alligators grow about eight to ten inches per year during their first five years, after which growth slows down. Females can attain nine feet in length, and males routinely reach up to 14 feet and weigh in at close to a thousand pounds. Female alligators and caimans are noticeably smaller than males, but there is less sexual dimorphism in crocodiles, so male and female crocodiles are similar in size. Female alligators grow much slower and do not live as long as males. In captivity, female alligators may reach 30 years; males can live past 60.

Horsepen Bayou•Photo credit: A. Brinly

Horsepen Bayou•Photo credit: A. Brinly

Texas alligators in coastal areas grow at a slower rate than those in other environments because of their different food sources. Coastal alligators mainly eat fish, while inland alligators consume more mammals and, therefore, more protein.

When alligators are submerged, it is difficult to estimate their length. If the head is visible, the distance in inches from the tip of the nose to the eye approximates the distance in feet from the tip of the nose to the end of the tail.

The longest recorded alligator, as the story goes, measured 19' 2" and was killed on Avery Island in Louisiana in 1890. The longest wild male alligator harvested in Texas measured 14' 8"—caught in Chalk Creek off the Trinity River. The longest wild female alligator in Texas measured 12 feet and was taken in Brazoria County.

V. History

PREHISTORIC

Crocodilians, birds, and dinosaurs all evolved from archosaurs. Indeed, crocodilians are structurally similar to birds in numerous ways, including having a muscular gizzard, an elongated outer-ear canal, and a complete separation of the ventricles in the heart. They also share similar behavior, such as nest-building and egg-laying.

Crocodilians (Crocodylia order) have been around for a long time. Reptiles, including crocodilians, evolved approximately one hundred million years ago, during the Cretaceous period.

During the long prehistoric past, the single continent known as Pangaea slowly split apart to form distinct continents, which resulted in the separation of the creatures that were around at the time. The split also resulted in a great divergence, through isolation among other factors, into many different species, as each evolved and adapted to their environment. Thus, today we have a range of crocodilians, as well as other animal groups, around the globe.

By the end of the Cretaceous period, around 65 million years ago, dinosaurs and many other creatures died out. But the crocodilians survived, as did the birds. In appearance and function, crocodilians have not changed that much over millions of years. The prehistoric crocodilians, however, were much larger than they are today—some 40 feet long. Bite marks of those beasts are found on the fossil remains of its dinosaur cousin Tyrannosaurus rex. The modern American alligator has been in existence for about two million years.

RECORDED HISTORY

The American alligator shows up in historical accounts of the sixteenth century, when Spanish explorers discovered them along the Gulf Coast. In fact, the Spanish word for lizard is *lagarto*, and was later changed by English-speaking people to "alligator."

Native Americans were hunting alligators for food when the Europeans arrived in North America. It has also been reported that early Native Americans would apply alligator fat to their bodies in attempts to protect themselves from mosquito bites.

Before Texas became a state, the Big Thicket area was called the alligator circuit. Itinerant Methodist preachers supplemented their incomes by killing alligators along the way and selling their hides in local towns.

Anahuac National Wildlife Refuge•Photo credit: William H. Powell

Alligators have been part of the Texas environment and culture long before—and after statehood. However, alligator populations began to decline once large numbers of people moved into the area.

Approaching Extinction

Many of the early settlers in Texas considered alligators a nuisance and killed them to protect livestock. Beginning in the mid-1800s, alligators were hunted for their hides, most of which were sent to France for production of leather goods. Tannery records indicate that at least ten million alligator hides were processed between 1870 and 1965.

Alligators were also killed for food, and alligator oil was used to lubricate machinery for the cotton industry. Large numbers of baby alligators were sold to tourists and shipped to pet stores in the north, where many of them died of pneumonia or calcium deficiency.

During the early 1960s, the only places alligators could be found in the wild were a few wildlife refuges and parks. In 1967, the American alligator was added to the endangered species list.

As alligator numbers were reduced and hunting limits were enacted, prices rose sharply for leather goods. Poaching became a million-dollar business. It was difficult to catch poachers, and, if they were caught and prosecuted, the fines were small and jail sentences short. It has been estimated that in 1968 the vast majority of all alligator goods came from illegal sources.

Traffic in alligator hides did not taper off until laws were passed to stop the tanners and marketers, as well. In 1969, New York passed the Mason-Smith Act, which banned the sale of endangered species and their products within the state. Other states, including Texas, enacted their own regulations protecting the alligator.

The Lacey Act, originally passed by the U.S. Congress in 1900, was amended in 1969 to prohibit interstate trade in hides obtained illegally. Unfortunately, these measures did not stop the slaughter of crocodilians. When domestic sources of alligator and crocodile hides were outlawed, dealers turned to caiman and crocodile hides exported from Central and South America, Africa, and Southeast Asia. The Lacey Act had made importing poached hides or those exported from illegal sources unlawful; yet, in the late 1960s and early '70s, American tanners were importing about 75,000 hides per year.

SURVIVAL

The Lacey Act was amended again in 1981 and 1988. The latter amendment created a separate violation for the intended falsification of documents pertaining to the exporting, importing, or transporting of wildlife. This amendment also included prosecution of commercial big-game guides who organized illegal hunts.

Today, the Lacey Act stands as one of the broadest and most comprehensive forces in the federal arsenal to combat wildlife crime. Under the act, violators are subject to criminal and civil penalties. The criminal penalty depends on the offender's conduct and the market value of the species at issue. For a felony, the maximum penalty is $20,000 and up to five years' imprisonment. For a misdemeanor, the maximum penalty is $10,000 and up to one year of imprisonment. Violators can also face forfeiture of any equipment used in the unlawful activity.

The Convention on International Trade in Endangered Species of Wild Fauna and Flora (CITES) is a multilateral treaty that outlaws trade in endangered animals and plants among member nations. The convention was drafted by members of the International Union for Conservation of Nature, and came into force in 1975. The United States is a member of CITES and, therefore, subject to its jurisdiction.

CITES controls the international trade of crocodilians and their products. By 1979, CITES had developed regulations to control the flow of non-endangered crocodilians, thereby allowing world trade of abundant species and disallowing trade of rare crocodilians. The author once purchased a crocodile belt while traveling in Australia and was given a CITES export permit, along with the receipt of payment.

CITES, however, does not protect habitat or how a species is used within a country.

Anahuac National Wildlife Refuge•Photo credit: Jill E. Krone

Congress enacted the Endangered Species Act (ESA) in 1973, a federal law that designates land necessary for the survival of a species as a critical habitat. The ESA further provides protection to endangered and threatened species to help prevent them from becoming extinct. ESA makes it illegal to import, export, take, possess, sell, or transport any endangered or threatened species.

A species or subspecies is endangered if it is "in danger of extinction throughout all or a significant portion of its range." A threatened species is one that is likely to become endangered in the foreseeable future.

ESA's provisions are enforced through citizen suits, as well as through criminal and civil penalties. A criminal violation may result in imprisonment and a fine of up to $50,000. If there is a criminal conviction, any equipment and vehicles that were used may be confiscated. A civil violation of a major provision may result in a fine up to $25,000.

Texas also passed its own Endangered Species Act in 1973.

As alligator populations increased, the alligator was removed from the endangered species list in 1987, making it one of only a handful of animals that has recovered from endangered status. The American alligator's survival is a tribute to modern conservation techniques, as well as federal and state cooperation.

Anahuac National Wildlife Refuge•Photo credit: William H. Powell

However, because several similar species of crocodiles and caimans are still in trouble, the U.S. Fish and Wildlife Service continues to regulate the legal trade in alligator skins and other products made from gators. The alligator is currently classified as "threatened due to similarity of appearance." The Service cooperates with state agencies, mainly the Texas Parks and Wildlife Department, in monitoring alligators in the state.

Today, the alligator in Texas is a protected game animal, and special permits are required to hunt, raise, or possess it.

VI. Hunting

Texas permits alligator hunting, which lends value to the animal. This in turn allows for more successful conservation of the gator and its habitat. At the same time, alligators are protected, and strict regulations limit their possession and sale.

The vast majority of Texas land is privately owned, but opportunities for hunting on public land are plentiful. Hunting is permitted on approximately 50 Wildlife Management Areas (WMAs) owned or operated by the Texas Parks and Wildlife Department. Hunting is also allowed on tracts owned by the Texas General Land Office, the U.S. Army Corps of Engineers, the U.S. Fish and Wildlife Service, the U.S. Forest Service, and by a number of other government agencies and private entities. Most of these areas, however, do not have alligators. Only half a dozen WMAs, for example, allow gator hunting.

Horsepen Bayou•Photo credit: A. Brinly

In the TPWD-designated alligator hunting "core counties" of Angelina, Brazoria, Calhoun, Chambers, Galveston, Hardin, Jackson, Jasper, Jefferson, Liberty, Matagorda, Nacogdoches, Newton, Orange, Polk, Refugio, Sabine, San Augustine, San Jacinto, Trinity, Tyler, and Victoria, the open alligator hunting season is September 10-30. This season also applies to any property, regardless of county, for which TPWD has issued hide tags directly to the landowner.

In all other counties, which are referred to as "non-core counties," open season for gator hunting is from April 1 through June 30.

A hunting license from the Texas Parks and Wildlife Department is required to hunt alligators in the state. Hunters can participate in TPWD's public hunting program if they do not have access to privately owned land. This program is comprised of "walk-in" hunting and the "drawn-hunt" system. In the walk-in hunting system, a licensed hunter can hunt anywhere that is open to alligator hunting during the season. In the drawn-hunt system, a licensed hunter can apply (on-line system) for a variety of supervised drawn hunts, including for exotic wildlife and quality native animals, on TPWD managed lands and specially leased private properties. Maps of public hunting lands are available from TPWD.

Anyone born on or after September 2, 1971, who wishes to hunt in Texas, must successfully complete a hunter-education training course. The course covers the regulations and responsibilities of hunting, safe firearm handling, outdoor survival skills, and wildlife conservation. TPWD, together with the Texas Wildlife Association, offers a hunting program for hunters age 16 and younger. This program highlights safety and education.

TPWD Wildlife Division conducts extensive studies in the state on the number, character, and harvest of alligators every year, in order to determine trends in the population, assess alligator habitat, and establish hunting limits. The Wildlife Division monitors the alligator population via aerial nest surveys and night eye-shine/ spotlight counts. Harvest recommendations for each season are determined by TPWD biologists, using a three-year average nest count, the percentage of adult alligators in a population, and a sustained-yield harvest rate.

Based on data acquired, TPWD allows not only the hunting of alligators, but also egg collection and farming activities (discussed in the section below).

Brazos Bend State Park•Photo credit: A. Brinly

If necessary, TPWD will suspend a hunting season. A sustained drought, for example, can reduce the alligator population to the point that harvesting them would negatively affect the population. On average, 1,200 alligators are taken annually in Texas.

TPWD publishes information on hunting on its website at www. tpwd.state.tx.us/huntwild/hunt/public. Information on alligator hunt-ing is also included in the recurrent *Outdoor Annual Hunting and*

Fishing Regulations. The more alligator-specific recurrent booklet, *Alligators in Texas: Rules, Regulations and General Information,* focuses on hunting. In addition to the regulations, including tagging and reporting requirements, TPWD material covers nuisance alligator protocol, skinning instructions, and alligator-related businesses, such as alligator buyers, hide tanners, and providers of alligator products and services. Required applications, as well as alligator-meat recipes, are included in TPWD material.

The tagging requirement is important. In order to take a wild alligator, the hunter must have obtained a tag from TPWD. This requirement has greatly reduced illegal hunting by making it difficult to sell or process an untagged alligator.

Texas has experienced a problem: the state is losing its large alligators (those ten feet or larger), which are crucial for maintaining a healthy population. Hunters with a limited number of tags tend to target the largest, most valuable alligators. Because it can take decades for an alligator to grow to ten-plus feet, removing too many of the big gators results in an explosion of small (three- to five-foot) alligators. The large alligators help expand the population and spread it more evenly, which prevents the smaller ones from overpopulating.

Enforcement of Hunting Regulations

The Texas Parks and Wildlife Department regulates hunting on state lands, as well as on private and federal lands.

The TPWD's Law Enforcement Division has a comprehensive statewide law enforcement program to protect Texas's wildlife, other natural resources, and the environment. The Division employs approximately 500 wardens throughout Texas and operates over two dozen field offices. Texas Game Wardens are responsible for enforcement of the Texas Parks and Wildlife Code, all TPWD regulations, and the Texas Penal Code, as well as selected statutes and regulations applicable to clean air and water, hazardous materials, and human health. Game wardens fulfill these responsibilities through educating the public about laws and regulations, by conducting high-visibility patrols, and by apprehending and arresting violators.

TPWD has a toll-free, 24/7 Operation Game Thief hotline (800-792-4263) for citizens to report poaching and other violations. Since it began in 1981, tens of thousands of calls have been received. Tipsters can receive rewards up to $1,000 for information leading to the arrest and conviction of a perpetrator of a wildlife crime. This privately funded program has paid out tens of thousands of dollars, and over a million dollars in fines have been assessed. Poaching violations can, of course, also be reported to local game wardens or to local police departments.

GATORFEST

Every year since 1989, the Texas Gatorfest has celebrated alligators and their habitats at Fort Anahuac Park, which is located in the town of Anahuac, overlooking Trinity Bay. However, after Hurricane Ike came ashore near Galveston in 2008, a twelve- to fifteen-foot storm surge along the upper Texas Gulf Coast cancelled that year's Gatorfest.

As part of the festival, the Great Texas Alligator Roundup (the premier event of Gatorfest) invites Texas gator hunters to bring in their catches to compete for cash prizes. The festival coincides with the opening of the area's 20-day alligator season, and the Roundup sees an average of 10% of the alligators annually harvested from the wild in Texas.

The town of Anahuac, which is the seat of Chambers County, was declared by the Texas Legislature in 1989 to be the Alligator Capital of Texas. Chambers County has approximately 35,000 people and 100,000 gators, which means that alligators outnumber people there three to one. Anahuac National Wildlife Refuge is home to a sizeable portion of that population.

VII. Farming

Florida and Louisiana dominate the alligator-farming industry, but there are a few operating farms in Texas. The Texas Parks and Wildlife Department publishes a booklet (*Alligator Farming in Texas*) that defines an alligator farmer as "any person who holds one or more live alligators in captivity for commercial purposes, including selling of alligators, eggs, hides, meat, or other parts of the alligator." TPWD also explains that the alligator-farming program is not intended for the "pet trade."

Each farm facility must be inspected before a permit is issued; those and other requirements are detailed in the TPWD booklet. Managing an alligator farm is expensive and requires a large capital investment, and a farmer may wait up to three years before generating income. However, compared to other animal industries, alligator farming requires small tracts of land, and does not have adverse effects on the environment when facilities are properly designed and operated.

Brazos Bend State Park•Photo credit: A. Brinly

The TPWD booklet lists acceptable sources of live alligators for farming, as well as egg-collection requirements. Import and export regulations are also discussed.

Alligators are farmed for their hides and meat, and usage is steadily increasing. Demand is well established in North America, Europe, and Asia. Most parts of farmed alligators are used for various markets, but their skins account for approximately 70% of their total wholesale value. Alligator skins are used to create a variety of products that range from fashion accessories to upholstery.

Farmed-raised alligator meat is low in fat and high in protein. With increasing human populations worldwide, it could become a more common food source. In Texas, the sale of alligator meat for human consumption is regulated by the Texas Department of State Heath Services. Facilities that process alligator meat must meet state regulations like those applicable to any meat processor.

The farmed-alligator supply chain typically begins in the marsh, with eggs laid by wild alligators. The portion of the eggs that farmers are permitted to collect is based on nest counts, habitat ratings, and population censuses. Regulations vary but are generally very strict concerning where, when, and how eggs may be collected. A permit is required to collect eggs in Texas.

Eggs are incubated on the farm, and hatchlings are raised in heated houses. In states other than Texas, the law may require some of the farmed alligators to be returned to where they were originally collected as eggs. The remaining animals are slaughtered for hides and meat.

After the animal is slaughtered, a tag is attached to the hide, and will not be removed until the hide becomes a finished leather product. A similar tagging system is used for meat products.

Farmed alligators compete in the marketplace with wild alligator harvests, as well as with crocodilians from South America and Asia. Farm-raised alligators are generally smaller than wild ones; typically, wild-harvested alligators average seven feet long and farm-raised alligators average four feet. The farmed alligator is harvested at four feet because it is not profitable to feed the animal beyond that.

Globally, crocodilians are a source of trade worth hundreds of millions annually. They also have a significant economic impact as tourist attractions. Indeed, ecotourism could be the best hope for saving endangered crocodilians, such as the critically endangered gharial, from extinction.

VIII. Alligator Tourism

Most Texas zoos have alligators on exhibit. However, there are other types of commercial and nonprofit facilities throughout the state that also exhibit alligators. If you want to see alligators in the wild, a number of nature parks and wildlife areas are open to the public. Some areas are wilder than others!

Brazos Bend State Park•Photo credit: A. Brinly

It is advised to obtain precise directions to the entrances of wildlife areas, as well as information on road conditions. Also inquire as to the location of any visitor centers, some of which are located off-site. Always check with authorities to find out the best areas to see alligators within a nature reserve. Some Wildlife Management Areas require permits and are only open for hunting and fishing; others are only open for wildlife viewing outside of hunting season. Some areas require a boat in order to view alligators.

The best time to see wild alligators is in the warm months and in the mornings, when they are more likely to be out of the water. Alligators are also active at dusk, but many nature parks close in the afternoon. Some nature facilities, however, allow camping.

It is important to ask about what particular precautions to take in the area to be visited, such as against poisonous snakes and poison ivy. See the "Warnings!" section below for more information on viewing alligators in the wild.

The following list of Texas nature reserves and other facilities, where the public can view alligators, is divided into geographic categories. Generally, the address listed is taken from the relevant website—and may not reflect the physical location of the nature reserve.

Northeastern Texas

•*Caddo Lake State Park and Wildlife Management Area*
245 Park Road 2/P.O. Box 226
Karnack, Texas 75661
State Park: 903-679-3351
WMA: 903-679-9817
www.tpwd.state.tx.us/state-parks
www.tpwd.state.tx.us/huntwild/hunt/wma/find_a_wma

•*East Texas Gators & Wildlife Park*
9515 FM 1255
Grand Saline, Texas 75140
903-962-5630
www.easttexasgators.com

•*Fort Worth Nature Center and Refuge*
9601 Fossil Ridge Road
Forth Worth, Texas 76135
817-392-7410
www.fwnaturecenter.org

•Gus Engeling Wildlife Management Area
16149 North US Hwy 287
Tennessee Colony, Texas 75861
903-928-2251
www.tpwd.state.tx.us/huntwild/hunt/wma/find_a_wma

•Richland Creek Wildlife Management Area
1670 FM 488
Streetman, Texas 75859
903-389-7080
www.tpwd.state.tx.us/huntwild/hunt/wma/find_a_wma

•Sabine National Forest
5050 Highway 21 East
Hemphill, Texas 75948
409-625-1940
www.fs.usda.gov/texas

Southeastern Texas

•Angelina-Neches/Dam B Wildlife Management Area
8096 FM 2782
Nacogdoches, Texas 75964
936-569-8547
www.tpwd.state.tx.us/huntwild/hunt/wma/find_a_wma

•B.A. Steinhagen Lake/Town Bluff Project
5171 FM 92 South
Woodville, Texas 75979
409-429-3491
www.swf-wc.usace.army.mil/townbluff

•Big Thicket National Preserve
6102 FM 420
Kountze, Texas 77625
409-951-6700
www.nps.gov/bith

•Huntsville State Park
P.O. Box 508
Huntsville, Texas 77342
936-295-5644
www.tpwd.state.tx.us/state-parks

•Lake Livingston State Park
300 Park Road 65
Livingston, Texas 77351
936-365-2201
www.tpwd.state.tx.us/state-parks

•Martin Dies, Jr. State Park
634 Park Road 48 South
Jasper, Texas 75951
409-384-5231
www.tpwd.state.tx.us/state-parks

•Roy E. Larsen Sandyland Sanctuary
3888 Highway 327
Silsbee, Texas 77656
409-658-2888
www.nature.org

•Sam Houston National Forest Wildlife Management Area
8096 FM 2782
Nacogdoches, Texas 75964
936-569-8547
www.tpwd.state.tx.us/huntwild/hunt/wma/find_a_wma

•Sam Rayburn Reservoir/Sam Rayburn Project
7696 RR 255 West
Jasper, Texas 75951
409-384-5716
www.swf-wc.usace.army.mil/samray

•*Village Creek State Park*
P.O. Box 8565
Lumberton, Texas 77657
409-755-7322
www.tpwd.state.tx.us/state-parks

Sabine Pass to Galveston

•*Anahuac National Wildlife Refuge*
4318 FM 1985
Anahuac, Texas 77514
409-267-3337
www.fws.gov/refuges

•*Gator Country Adventure Park*
21159 FM 365 (at I-10 (Exit 838))
Beaumont, Texas 77705
409-794-9453
www.gatorrescue.com

•*J.D. Murphree Wildlife Management Area*
10 Parks & Wildlife Drive
Port Arthur, Texas 77640
409-736-2551
www.tpwd.state.tx.us/huntwild/hunt/wma/find_a_wma

•*Lower Neches Wildlife Management Area*
10 Parks & Wildlife Drive
Port Arthur, Texas 77640
409-736-2551
www.tpwd.state.tx.us/huntwild/hunt/wma/find_a_wma

•*McFaddin National Wildlife Refuge*
P.O. Box 358
Sabine Pass, Texas 77655
409-971-2909
www.fws.gov/refuges

•*Sabine Pass Battleground State Historic Site*
6100 Dowling Road
Port Arthur, Texas 77655
512-463-7948/409-332-8820
www.thc.state.tx.us

•*Sea Rim State Park*
19335 S. Gulfway Drive
Sabine Pass, Texas 77655
409-971-2559
www.tpwd.state.tx.us/state-parks

•*Shangri La Botanical Gardens and Nature Center*
2111 West Park Avenue
Orange, Texas 77630
409-670-9113
www.shangrilagardens.org

•*Smith Oaks Bird Sanctuary*
End of Old Mexico Road
High Island, Texas 77623
713-932-1639
www.houstonaudubon.org

•*Texas Point National Wildlife Refuge*
P.O. Box 358
Sabine Pass, Texas 77655
409-971-2909
www.fws.gov/refuges

•*Tony Houseman Wildlife Management Area*
8096 FM 2782
Nacogdoches, Texas 75964
936-569-8547
www.tpwd.state.tx.us/huntwild/hunt/wma/find_a_wma

•Trinity River Island Recreation Area/Wallisville Lake Project
1140 US Army Corps Road
Wallisville, Texas 77597
409-389-2285
www.swg.usace.army.mil

•Trinity River National Wildlife Refuge
601 FM 1011
Liberty, Texas 77575
936-336-9786
www.fws.gov/refuges

Houston area

•Armand Bayou Nature Center
8500 Bay Area Blvd.
Pasadena, Texas 77507
281-474-2551
www.abnc.org

•Lake Houston Wilderness Park
25840 FM 1485
New Caney, Texas 77357
281-354-6881
www.houstontx.gov/parks/ourparks/lakehoustonpark.html

•Sheldon Lake State Park and Environmental Learning Center
14140 Garrett Road
Houston, Texas 77044
281-456-2800
www.tpwd.state.tx.us/state-parks

•Brazoria National Wildlife Refuge
24907 FM 2004
Angleton, Texas 77515
979-922-1037
www.fws.gov/refuges

•Brazos Bend State Park
21901 FM 762
Needville, Texas 77461
979-553-5102
www.tpwd.state.tx.us/state-parks

•Crocodile Encounter
23231 County Road 48
Angleton, Texas 77515
281-595-2232
http://thecrocodileexperience.com

•Guadalupe Delta Wildlife Management Area
2200 7th Street, 3rd Floor
Bay City, Texas 77414
361-552-6637
www.tpwd.state.tx.us/huntwild/hunt/wma/find_a_wma

•Mad Island Wildlife Management Area
2200 7th Street, 3rd Floor
Bay City, Texas 77414
979-323-9579
www.tpwd.state.tx.us/huntwild/hunt/wma/find_a_wma

•Redhead Pond Wildlife Management Area
County Courthouse, Room 101
Bay City, Texas 77414
979-323-9553
www.tpwd.state.tx.us/huntwild/hunt/wma/find_a_wma

•San Bernard National Wildlife Refuge
6801 County Road 306
Brazoria, Texas 77422
979-964-3639
www.fws.gov/refuges

•Texana Park
(Lavaca Navidad River Authority)
46 Park Road 1
Edna, Texas 77957
361-782-5718
www.brackenridgepark.com

Between Port Lavaca and Corpus Christi

•Aransas National Wildlife Refuge
P.O. Box 100
Austwell, Texas 77950
361-286-3559
www.fws.gov/refuges

•Goose Island State Park
202 S. Palmetto Street (near Lamar)
Rockport, Texas 78382
361-729-2858
www.tpwd.state.tx.us/state-parks

•Leonabelle Turnbull Birding Center
Ross Avenue (behind the Trolley Stop)
Port Aransas, Texas 78373
361-749-4158
www.port-aransas.net/leona_belle_turnbull_birding_center.aspx

•Welder Wildlife Foundation and Refuge
10429 Welder Wildlife
Sinton, Texas 78387
361-364-2643
www.welderwildlife.org

Corpus Christi area

•Hans & Pat Suter Wildlife Refuge
6000 Ennis Joslin Road
Corpus Christi, Texas 78412
361-826-3460
http://visitcorpuschristitx.org/hans_pat_suter_wildlife_refuge.cfm

Corpus Christi to San Antonio

•Choke Canyon State Park
P.O. Box 2
Calliham, Texas 78007
361-786-3868
www.tpwd.state.tx.us/state-parks

•James E. Daughtrey Wildlife Management Area
64 Chaparral WMA Drive
Cotulla, Texas 78014
830-676-3413
www.tpwd.tx.us/huntwild/hunt/wma/find_a_wma

Rio Grande Valley

•Estero Llano Grande State Park
3301 S. International Blvd. (FM 1015)
Weslaco, Texas 78596
956-565-3919
www.tpwd.state.tx.us/state-parks

•Harlingen Arroyo Colorado
(Hugh Ramsey Nature Park)
1001 S. Loop 499
Harlingen, Texas 78550
956-427-8873
www.theworldbirdingcenter.com/harlingen.html

•Laguna Atascosa National Wildlife Refuge
22688 Buena Vista Blvd.
Los Fresnos, Texas 78566
956-748-3607
www.fws.gov/refuges

•South Padre Island Birding and Nature Center
6801 Padre Boulevard
South Padre Island, TX 78597
956-761-6801
http://southpadreislandbirding.com

Volunteers

Texas state parks and other nature facilities are always looking for volunteers, and some hire interns. If you wish to get more involved in protecting alligators and other wildlife, this would be a hands-on way to do so. Programs throughout the state offer a broad range of volunteer options that can be tailored to fit individual talents, experience, and time frames. The Texas Parks and Wildlife Department reports that, annually, its volunteers donate more than a half-million hours of service—amounting to more than $17,000,000 to the Department. For more information, contact www.tpwd.state.tx.us/involved/volunteer.

For federal parks and other nature facilities, contact the facility directly for more information on volunteering.

IX. Warnings!

Alligators are fascinating animals, but they are also dangerous and capable of inflicting serious injury or death to humans. Even baby alligators bite.

The Texas Parks and Wildlife Department reports that alligator complaints are increasing. In spite of the increase, there have been few reported alligator-caused injuries statewide in recent years. There has been only one fatality in modern times. In July 2015, a young man unfortunately drowned in Adam's Bayou in Orange, Texas, after he was attacked by a 400 lb. alligator. The nighttime attack caused major trauma to the victim's left arm, and puncture wounds were found in his upper left chest area. Part of the man's left arm was found in the gator's stomach.

Anahuac National Wildlife Refuge•Photo credit: William H. Powell

Florida, on the other hand, has a tally of 22 fatal alligator attacks—since 1948—including an attack on a burglar who was hiding from the police at the water's edge of Barefoot Bay. When the man's body was discovered, the victim was missing parts of both legs and an arm. Interestingly, Louisiana has a larger gator population than Florida, but does not experience many alligator attacks. This, no doubt, is due to fewer people living in the state's gator habitats.

Early Texas history also reveals stories of fatal alligator attacks. In the 1600s, a servant of the French explorer La Salle was killed by a large alligator while he was swimming in the Colorado River. In 1836, a Mr. King, who was traveling with a group of settlers fleeing Santa Anna's army after the fall of the Alamo, was killed by an adult alligator while he was crossing the Trinity River.

Golf course in Friendswood, Texas•Photo credit: Tony Arcangeli

TPWD reports that the increase in human-alligator encounters is mainly due to residential and business development infringing on alligator habitats. At the same time, alligators are expanding their range in Texas.

People are more likely to encounter an alligator in the springtime, when alligators are most active, looking for new territory and to reproduce. Periods of extreme weather conditions, such as drought or heavy rains, can also trigger them to relocate.

Fishermen and even golfers are likely to encounter alligators, as the author's two nephews can attest. If your golf ball lands in that innocent-looking pond, it is best not to try and retrieve it!

Armand Bayou•Photo credit: A. Brinly

Fishermen frequently encounter alligators because gators will pursue top-water fishing lures that look like food. Most alligators can be easily scared away, but some nuisance alligators will repeatedly follow boats at a close distance without submerging. Fish scraps should be disposed of, not thrown in the water or left on shore, in order to discourage any connection between humans and food.

It is recommended that you keep at least 30 feet away from an alligator. It is also prudent to avoid alligator nests, as the mother gator may be near. It should not be assumed that the animal is slow or lethargic. In fact, they can run up to 35 miles per hour for short distances on land. If an alligator hisses, it is a warning that you are too close. Retreat slowly, making no quick moves.

If you are in areas where alligators are found, it is important to keep children close and make sure pets are on leashes.

Never swim or wade where alligators are present. If you see something in the water that looks like a half-sunken log, it could be an alligator. They can lie like this for hours, perfectly motionless.

The Texas Parks and Wildlife Department reminds us that alligators can be killed in "immediate defense" of human life, or to protect domestic animals and livestock. Such a defensive killing must be reported to TPWD within 24 hours.

TPWD explains that encounters with nuisance alligators should also be reported. A nuisance alligator is an alligator that is killing livestock or pets, or is a threat to human health and safety. Not all alligator encounters, however, need to be reported—only those that would result in harm to humans, pets, or livestock. TPWD seeks to teach civilians to recognize the few nuisance alligators and coexist safely with the rest of them.

Primary responsibility for resolving alligator nuisances rests with the TPWD's Law Enforcement Division. The U.S. Fish and Wildlife Service, local animal control officers, and wildlife rescue/rehabilitation personnel assist TPWD in responding to requests for assistance with nuisance alligators.

When an alligator becomes a nuisance, it may have to be relocated by the proper authorities, and sometimes killed. Relocation can create greater problems, because alligators are territorial and tend to return to their home territory.

Nuisance alligators have often been fed by people and have lost their natural fear of humans. TPWD specifically warns the public not to feed a wild alligator or allow it to get food. In October 2003, it became a Class C misdemeanor, punishable by a fine of $25-$500, to intentionally feed a free-ranging alligator. It is also a violation of state law to remove any alligator from its natural environment or to accept one as a pet. Alligators do not become tame in captivity!

X. Protection of the Alligator

Protection of the wild alligator requires protection of its habitat, and there are 3,700 named streams and 15 major rivers that run through the Texas landscape. These aquatic ecosystems play a major role not only in the protection of the alligator and other wildlife, but also are crucial to the health of the state's economy.

Horsepen Bayou•Photo credit: A. Brinly

Water that eventually flows into the seven major estuaries of the state (Aransas/Copano Bay, Corpus Christi/Nueces Bay, Galveston Bay, Matagorda Bay, Sabine Lake, San Antonio Bay, and Upper and Lower Laguna Madre) supports over 212 reservoirs, countless riparian habitats, wetlands, and terrestrial areas. Programs have been created to help preserve these areas, such as the Galveston Bay Estuary Program, a Texas Commission on Environmental Quality project, which also offers volunteer opportunities and workshops. The Galveston Bay Foundation is an example of a non-profit organization that was established to protect and enhance Galveston Bay.

The Texas Parks and Wildlife Department's State Wetlands Conservation Plan encourages and supports landowners who want to protect and restore wetlands on their properties. The Texas Parks and Wildlife Foundation has created the Lone Star Legacy Endowment Fund to provide funds for every state park, wildlife area, historical site, and fish hatchery in the state. Donating to the endowment fund ensures the health of Texas park programs. The Texas Recreation and Park Society also supports the state's parks. There are other Texas conservation organizations that contribute to the well-being of wildlife.

As mentioned above, the federal government has supported wetlands protection and restoration in Texas, through the U.S. Fish and Wildlife Service, the U.S. Environmental Protection Agency, and the U.S. Army Corps of Engineers. Many national refuges have non-profit volunteer organizations associated with them, such as the Friends of Anahuac Refuge that supports the Anahuac National Wildlife Refuge. Texas also benefits from support from nationwide non-profits that are engaged in protecting wildlife and habitats.

The Texas Master Naturalist program is a nature-based volunteer organization. Master Naturalists volunteer for a multitude of projects, including ones involving urban wildlife. This program is available to anyone over 18 years old, and provides both field and classroom training.

If volunteering or joining a conservation or wildlife association is not feasible, the private citizen can, of course, visit nature reserves. During the 2011 drought and wildfires, visits to state parks dramatically decreased, leading to an almost $5 million budget shortfall. It is critical that Texans visit their nature reserves and make donations, in order to prevent the loss of park jobs and keep parks from closing completely.

All of us can do something as simple as not littering, as this illegal practice harms alligators and other wild animals. Alligators will eat almost anything, including glass bottles, metallic objects, or anything that looks edible to them.

American alligators are highly successful animals, and are today contributing to a healthy Texas wilderness and to promising research. These animals deserve our respect and our protection.

Anahuac National Wildlife Refuge•Photo credit: William H. Powell

References

Bartlett, R.D., and Patricia Bartlett. *Guide and Reference to the Crocodilians, Turtles, and Lizards of Eastern and Central North America (North of Mexico)*. 1st ed. Gainesville, Florida: University Press of Florida, 2006. Print.

Dallas Zoo. "Ghosts from the Bayou Move the Spirit." Dallas Zoo News Release. Dallas, Texas: Dallas Zoo, 2009. Print.

Favre, David, Rebecca Wisch, and et al, eds. "Statutes/Laws: Texas." Animal Legal and Historical Center. Michigan State University College of Law, November 2013. Web. 20 March 2014.

<http://www.animallaw.info/statutes/stustxparks_wild_65_001.htm>

Foster, William C. *Historic Native Peoples of Texas*. 1st ed. Austin, Texas: University of Texas Press, 2008. Print.

Hodge, Larry D. *Official Guide to Texas Wildlife Management Areas*. 1st ed. Austin, Texas: Texas Parks and Wildlife Press. 2000. Print.

Hogan, Dan, Michele Hogan, and et al, eds. "Gator in Your Tank: Alligator Fat as a New Source of Biodiesel Fuel." *ScienceDaily*. ScienceDaily, LLC., 17 August 2011. Web. 20 March 2014. [See source report in the American Chemical Society's journal, *Industrial & Engineering Chemistry Research*, 2011.]

<http://www.sciencedaily.com/releases/2011/08/110817094926.htm>

Lockwood, C.C. *The Alligator Book*. 1st ed. Baton Rouge, Louisiana: Louisiana State University Press, 2002. Print.

Lutz, Greg C. *Alligator Profile*. Agricultural Marketing Resource Center. Iowa State University, April 2012. Web. April 2012.

<http://www.agmrc.org/commodities_products/aquaculture/alligator-profile>

Ray, David A. "Sequencing Three Crocodilian Genomes to Illuminate the Evolution of Archosaurs and Amniotes." *Genome Biology*. 13.1(2012). Web. 20 March 2014.

<http://genomebiology.com/2012/13/1/415#>

Rue, III. Leonard Lee. *Alligators and Crocodiles*: *A Portrait of the Animal World*. New York, New York: Todtri Productions, 1994. Print.

Toops, Connie M. *The Alligator: Monarch of the Marsh*. Homestead, Florida: Florida National Parks & Monuments Association, Inc., 1988. Print.

About the Author

Darlene Prescott, born in Houston, is an attorney licensed in New York and Texas. She is on the board of the Friends of Anahuac Refuge, and is an active member of the Armand Bayou Nature Center in Pasadena, Texas, where she now lives. She wants to see wildlife thrive in natural habitats around the world.

Anahuac National Wildlife Refuge•Photo credit: Jill E. Krone

She has since childhood had a special interest in reptiles of all types. One day while browsing in a bookstore, Darlene noticed that there were books on Texas wildflowers, trees, insects, fishes, and even reptiles, but no specific book on Texas alligators. So she decided to write one.

Darlene, having worked for the United Nations for 28 years in New York—with two overseas U.N. peacekeeping assignments in Lebanon and East Timor (now Timor-Leste)—has had articles on public international law published. Various Texas newspapers have carried her articles on alligators. Darlene has also dabbled in fiction writing, and won Honorable Mention in a nationwide short story writing contest in 2010. She is currently writing a novel and performing pro bono work in the Houston area.

REQUEST FOR FEEDBACK

The author would greatly appreciate any constructive feedback on the book, including information on other sites where the public can view alligators, for future editions of this book.

Please submit to dprescottxgators@gmail.com.

Thank you.

Anahuac National Wildlife Refuge: See you later ....•Photo credit: Darlene Prescott

Made in the USA
San Bernardino, CA
21 March 2016